CRAZY
LAWSUIT STORIES

Discover 101 of The Most Bizarre, Hilarious, and Mind-Boggling Lawsuits Ever!

Gavin Barnett

ISBN: 978-1-962496-03-2

FREE BONUS

SCAN ME!

GET OUR NEXT BOOK FOR FREE!
Scan or go to:
OakHarborPress.com/Free

Table of Contents

INTRODUCTION

A significant advantage of a democratic government, like that in the U.S., is a well-established judicial system. It gives citizens the opportunity to seek justice through the courts. However, the drawback is that some people use this opportunity to file cases that are strange, outlandish, and so absurd that they leave onlookers shaking their heads. Some of these peculiar cases have merit, while others are what most people consider litigious, if not outright unjust. Most of these unusual lawsuits are dismissed by the judges overseeing the cases and end up as late-night comedy topics.

The majority of these lawsuits stem from what most people would describe as minor or negligible inconveniences. Some of them concern marketing claims taken too literally or out of context. Other cases are between companies, such as one claiming the other has imitated their recipe, motto, or advertisement campaign. In this book, there are 101 weird lawsuits that will surprise and entertain you, many of which are hard to believe truly happened.

1

WHERE'S THE MOZZARELLA?

A woman named Amy Joseph sued the makers of *TGI Friday's* mozzarella sticks after claiming the snacks contained cheddar cheese and not mozzarella. She claimed the appetizer makers were unfair, deceptive, and unlawful. Additionally, she argued that most customers decide to purchase *TGI Friday's* mozzarella sticks because they believe they're made with mozzarella cheese. According to Joseph, who bought the products on Amazon in January 2021, the products were essentially worthless, and she got what she didn't bargain for.

Her lawyer claimed that the snack manufacturers should include "imitation" on the bag so that customers know they're not made with mozzarella and that this information doesn't appear anywhere on the package. Reportedly, if the plaintiff had known the snacks weren't made with mozzarella, she wouldn't have purchased them at all. The lawsuit also made mention of various health benefits of mozzarella (lower calories, sodium, and fats) compared to other cheeses, making it a more desirable option. The lawsuit also stated that the term "mozzarella sticks" should only refer to food that has mozzarella cheese as the primary ingredient. The lawsuit sought unspecified "actual, punitive, enhanced and statutory damages" and restitution of inequitable money obtained by the Defendants. In December 2021, a judge ruled for the case to move forward but removed *TGI Friday's* from the lawsuit.

Interestingly, this is just one of several lawsuits filed against snack companies that claim to contain a particular cheese but actually lack that ingredient.

2

POP-TARTS
FOUND LACKING

Although a lot of us know that Kellogg's Pop-Tarts contain loads of sugar, there was a lawsuit filed attacking the company for presenting them as a healthy food. An Illinois resident, Anita Harris, filed a $5 million lawsuit against Pop-Tarts for misleading the public into believing the treat contains more strawberries than it actually does. The lawsuit also emphasized the health benefits of strawberries, including guarding against certain cancers, increasing good cholesterol, lowering blood pressure, and providing protection to the cardiovascular system.

Harris argued that the name "Frosted Strawberry Toaster Pastries" was misleading, false, and deceptive to consumers purchasing the product and that it contains more pears and apples than it does strawberries. According to Harris, other toaster pastries like Walmart's Great Value brand and Dollar Tree's Clover Value brand use the phrase "natural and artificial" on their packaging to make it known to consumers that the product might not contain real, whole strawberries. Pop-Tart boxes don't contain any such phrases to warn consumers about what they are purchasing.

3

NO CHEESE, PLEASE

In 2018, Florida couple Leonard Werner and Cynthia Kissner filed a $5 million lawsuit over cheese. It is fairly common for people to order a McDonald's Quarter Pounder with cheese, and even when mistakes are made, people usually just move on or immediately amend the situation by asking for a replacement item. However, Werner and Kissner took McDonald's to court over being charged the price of a Quarter Pounder with cheese when they specifically asked for no cheese.

The couple claimed that they were forced to pay the same amount for the extra dairy. They argued that the price of hamburgers and cheeseburgers differ on the McDonald's menu. The lawsuit claimed that McDonald's used to have four different versions of the Quarter Pounder on the menu, two of which came with cheese and the other two without cheese that cost between 30 and 90 cents. However, the fast-food chain stopped selling the four different Quarter Pounders and now has just one on their menu list; and the ingredients listed for that one include cheese.

The couple claims to have suffered an injury because they were overcharged. The case was dismissed when the judge determined the couple was not harmed by paying for the extra slices of cheese and noted that the franchise had no policies promising customers such alterations to the menu items.

4

FAKE FIGHTER
JET PRIZE

Although this lawsuit happened in the '90s, it is still among the most famous cases in the world. In 1996, Pepsi, the carbonated drink company, made a silly mistake when advertising a "Pepsi point" scheme. They launched a marketing campaign where customers saved up Pepsi labels to redeem prizes from the company. Most of the prizes were articles of clothing with the company's logo on them. During the launch, there was a commercial in which the company jokingly stated that anyone who collected 7 million labels could receive a new Harrier jump jet.

John Leonard was a student at the time who thought he had found a clever way to earn himself that Harrier jump jet. John convinced a millionaire named Todd Hoffman to lend him the $700,000 needed to acquire 7 million labels. When John attempted to collect this massive prize, worth $23 million, from Pepsi, he was promptly denied.

The young man hired a lawyer and sued the company. Pepsi claimed the advert was clearly a joke, and out of the millions of people who watched, John was the only person who tried to redeem the offer. In later years, the lawsuit inspired the Netflix series *Pepsi, Where's My Jet?*

5

NOT ENOUGH NAPKINS

Webster Lucas sued the local McDonald's in Los Angeles, CA, for not giving him enough napkins. When he only received a single napkin at the franchise and was denied any more, he took the matter to court. The situation, though, was ostensibly not about the napkins at all but about the way Lucas was treated while requesting more. When the manager was called to mediate the situation, Lucas told him he would have instead gone to eat at Jack-in-the-Box (another food service provider) to avoid arguing over napkins and just enjoy his meal. According to Lucas, the manager, who was reportedly a Latino man, made a racially discriminating remark by referring to him as "you people." He strongly believed the manager used the phrase because he is African American.

After the incident, Mr. Lucas emailed the McDonald's general manager claiming that the napkin incident prevented him from working because he was suffering from "mental anguish." To compensate for the discomfort, the general manager offered him free burgers, which he refused. Instead, he sued them for $1.5 million.

6

FEAR WAS A FACTOR

Austin Aitken, a 49-year-old man from Cleveland, sued NBC for an episode of one of their popular TV shows, *Fear Factor*. *Fear Factor* was a game show with seven seasons in which contestants faced their worst fears. The contestants were made to go through a series of challenges that ranged from gross to terrifying to win a grand prize.

In one of the *Fear Factor* episodes, the contestants were challenged to eat rats mixed in a blender. This was the episode Aitken sued NBC over, asking for $2.5 million as compensation. According to Aitken, he had no problem with contestants eating insects and worms for the $50,000 prize, as seen in other episodes, but eating rats was too much. He claimed that the episode caused his blood pressure to rise, which made him feel lightheaded and dizzy. It even made him vomit. Watching people consume blended rats caused disorientation, and he ended up running into a door.

This is why Aitken sued for suffering. The executive producer of the show, Matt Kunitz, in defense, drew attention to the point of the show — to make people face their fears. The case ended with a dismissal, as it was considered frivolous.

7

BARRELS OF CORN SYRUP

In 2019, Anheuser-Busch, producer of Bud Light and other beers, aired Superbowl commercials insinuating that MillerCoors used corn syrup in their Coors Light and Miller Lite beers. This led to a lengthy lawsuit under the pretenses of interfering with sales and creating advertisements that were "false and misleading."

The advertisement featured a king of the fictitious Bud Light Castle receiving the wrong barrel of ale, which contained corn syrup. The king returned the barrel to its rightful owner—the king of the Coors Light castle. MillerCoors did not take the jibe lightly. In court, MillerCoors argued that there was no corn syrup in their product and that it was actually Bud Light that used corn syrup during the fermentation process. The vice president of Anheuser-Busch, Gemma Hart, said the campaign was intended to show the difference between Coors Light and Miller Lite. After months of legal proceedings, the case was eventually overturned.

8

THE WRONG
KIND OF SWEET

In 2022, Missy Baker and her attorney, Spencer Sheehan, filed a lawsuit against Walmart's Great Value brand honey mustard in Illinois. The plaintiff claimed that the honey mustard had sugar as its primary sweetener, not honey. The largest issue was that the dressing's packaging displayed a picture of a honey dipper with the phrasing "Made with Real Honey," leading consumers to believe the honey mustard contained more wholesome ingredients than other brands.

According to the ingredient list on the product, honey is not the primary sweetener. The lawsuit stated that fewer customers would pay the product's price if it was not for the misleading packaging. Baker sought monetary damages as well as a re-branding of the product to represent its ingredients accurately.

9

FAKE CINNAMON
IN THE MINTS

Mars, Inc., producer of Altoids mints, was brought to court by Brent Scruggs in 2022 over the packaging of their product. The mints are sold in a small tin case that displays cinnamon sticks on the front. Despite the insinuation that the product is made with cinnamon, it is not in the ingredient list.

Furthermore, the lawsuit clearly stated the federal government's rule, which stipulates that when a label makes use of any primary flavor, and it contains artificial components, the flavor name must be accompanied by the prefix "artificial" or "artificially flavored" boldly on the product's label.

Scruggs looked for enough compensation to cover the legal fees as well as compensation for being misled by the packaging.

10

UNDERFILLED JUNIOR MINTS

Trekeela Perkins from Mississippi and Biola Daniel and Abel Duran from New York filed a lawsuit against Tootsie Roll Industries about Junior Mints boxes being only partially filled. Many people have encountered this when purchasing boxes of candy, finding that almost half of the box is filled with air rather than the purchased treats. Junior Mints are small round chocolates with mint filling, introduced in 1949. The chocolate candy gained attention in 1993 on the TV show *Seinfeld* and has since flourished in popularity, often found in movie theaters and grocery stores.

In their defense, Tootsie Roll stated that a slack-fill is the space difference between a box/packaging and the actual volume of the product in it. They also noted that federal law allows for some slack-fill for the contents' protection and enough space for the product to settle when shipping to a far destination.

In the end, the judge decided there was no fraud because the customers could determine the actual quantity based on the weight listed on the package.

11

FIREFIGHTER AFRAID OF FIGHTING FIRES

When disaster strikes, firefighters are real-life heroes who help save lives and properties from a wide variety of circumstances. These professionals sign up, fully aware of the dangers their jobs demand. Shayne Proler was the captain of a Houston, Texas, fire department, and in 2004, he answered a call that would forever change his career. After entering a building that was on fire, the captain was left with a terrible fear of fire.

In 2006, he was in another position to enter a home that was on fire. With the trauma of his previous experience still affecting him, he became disoriented. His peers reported him struggling to put on his gear, talk, and even walk. The captain was removed from the team tasked with handling fire suppression and instead was sent back to the academy for more training. Proler worked hard to get back on active duty against the wishes of his fire department. This fight worked its way into court. Proler sued the fire department, claiming that their refusal to allow him onto active duty was a violation of the Americans with Disabilities Act. The jury favored Proler's position, and he was awarded $362,000 to cover the legal fees associated with the lawsuit.

12

KIDNAPPER SUES HOSTAGES

One of the stranger lawsuits out there is a case where a kidnapper sued his hostages. In 2009, Jesse Dimmick was on the run after beating a Colorado man to death. He burst into the Rowleys' home and threatened them at knife-point. The altercation ended in a shootout with the police.

In the aftermath, the Rowleys filed a case with the Shawnee County District Court, suing Jesse Dimmick for $75,000 in reparations for the emotional damage they suffered from the home invasion. This was when Dimmick decided to file a counter lawsuit, requesting $235,000 in compensation to cover the hospital bills incurred during the shootout with the cops on the grounds, saying that they breached an oral contract that had been formed during the home invasion.

When the police arrived at the Rowleys' home, Jesse Dimmick was scared for his life and pleaded for the couple to hide him. He offered the couple an unspecified amount of money in exchange for help, which entered them into a verbal contract. The Rowleys brought Dimmick over to their neighbor's house to hide him from the police, where he ate snacks, watched movies, and eventually fell asleep. This was the point at which the couple and the neighbors were able to escape from Dimmick.

In 2010, Dimmick was convicted of four felonies (including two kidnappings) and sentenced to 10 years and 11 months in jail. Later on, Dimmick was sent to a Brighton, Colorado jail for about eight charges, including murder, and no plea has been entered since then.

The Rowleys' attorney filed a motion denying the oral contract claimed by the kidnapper. He said that even if there was a contract, it was forged under duress while Jesse Dimmick held them hostage at knife-point. The argument was that anyone would agree to help under those circumstances, and therefore the contract was null and void.

13

MICHAEL JORDAN LOOK-ALIKE

It is not uncommon for athletes to face or file lawsuits, sometimes intentionally going to court for the sake of gaining the public's attention. In 2006, Allen Heckard grabbed the spotlight when he sued Michael Jordan for $832 million on the premise that Michael Jordan looked too much like Heckard, and it was impacting his daily life.

Allen Heckard claims that for 15 years, he was repeatedly mistaken for being Michael Jordan, and he was tired and fed up with the situation. The lawsuit sued Michael Jordan and Phil Knight (founder of Nike) for the combined amount. If you're wondering why Mr. Knight was mentioned, it is for promoting Jordan to become one of the most famous men worldwide. Jordan was accused of defamation and inflicting permanent injury, emotional suffering, and pain. Knight was charged with defamation and permanent injury.

When asked why he demanded that outrageous amount, Heckard said he multiplied his age by seven and came up with the number. How strange! He went ahead to pay $209 for legal fees to start the process, but the legal proceedings and case were dismissed without amounting to anything. It's possible that a lot of people would be glad to look like and be mistaken for Jordan for free, unlike Heckard.

14

ALL OUT OF
CHICKEN SANDWICHES

In 2019, Craig Barr entered a Popeyes Louisiana Kitchen in Chattanooga, Tennessee. He was after the heavily advertised chicken sandwiches, which were, unfortunately, out of stock. Barr demanded $5,000 and accused Popeyes of "false advertisement" and "deceptive business practices by entities to the public."

Craig Barr said he suffered emotional damage, wasted his time, and required compensation for damage to his car. In his search for a Popeyes chicken sandwich, Barr traveled to multiple restaurant locations, all of which were out of chicken sandwiches, and asked him to return the following day. He claimed that one of the parking lots was dangerous enough to cause potential injury. Barr told *Chattanooga Times Free Press* that he was not happy because he had the sandwich on his mind and was unable to think straight without having it. Even though he filed a lawsuit against the fast-food chain, he said he'd still buy one of the sandwiches when the item returned to the menu.

Popeyes, in their defense, said they had planned for enough stock to last them six weeks but unexpectedly sold out in two weeks. They further stated that their sales skyrocketed because of the social media engagement they received due to an online Twitter debate that erupted regarding which restaurant carried the best chicken sandwich.

Though you'd be sad if you found out that the sandwich you craved was sold out, would you care enough to take it to court?

15

A FINGER IN
WENDY'S CHILI

The scam pulled by Anna Aayala of San Jose made people think twice before purchasing a cup of chili from Wendy's. In 2005, Aayala falsely claimed she saw a human finger in her chili. The scam made a lot of international headlines and, to this day, has left its mark as a commonly shared urban legend. This false allegation cost the fast-food chain an estimated $21 million in total loss of business as a result of the case.

Aayala and her husband Jaime Plascencia pleaded guilty to attempting to scam the fast-food chain. Aayala confessed to cooking the fingertip in a pot at her Las Vegas home. She drove all the way to San Jose and dipped it into the chili. The severed finger was supplied by Aayala's husband, who had obtained it from a coworker who lost it in an industrial accident. Aayala publicly warned patrons to avoid the chili. All efforts to get a comment from the chain's representative proved futile after Aayala's scam. Aayala was sentenced to four years in prison, and Brian Rossiter, the guy whose finger was used, was paid $100 for the severed finger. Aayala's husband is still serving his sentence. Neither are allowed to return to Wendy's again.

Aayala was released on good behavior after serving a year in prison. After serving her term, she told reporters that during her jail time, she was ridiculed by both officials and inmates who called her the "Finger Lady" in the penitentiary. Even after serving her term, she is still known by the nickname.

16

C+ IS NOT
GOOD ENOUGH

Megan Thode, a graduate student, sued her professor and Lehigh University in Bethlehem, Pennsylvania, for awarding her a C+ grade in one of her classes. She claimed the mediocre grade was a hindrance to achieving her goals. Thode had always desired a degree to become a licensed therapist. In response to the grade, Megan Thode sued for monetary damages, seeking $1.3 million in lost earnings and an official grade change. She claimed that the C+ prevented her, an otherwise A student, from taking further classes and sabotaged her degree. The low grade resulted in Thode settling for a master's degree in human development, contrary to her initial ambitions.

The case was filed in Northampton county court. Judge Emil Giordano declined to dismiss the suit and ruled that the case had enough evidence for proceedings. Megan Thode took the class in the fall of 2009, and her instructor, Amanda Eckhardt, said she stood by the given grade and that Thode acted unprofessionally, which earned her a zero out of 25 points for class participation. Her instructor believed she got the grade she deserved with the behavior she exhibited. Thode's attorney, Richard Orloski, argued that Thode's open advocacy for gay marriage could be the reason why Eckhardt targeted her. Eckhardt testified that she believed marriage should be strictly between a man and a woman. Furthermore, she said her beliefs are personal and don't affect how she treats her students. She told the court that Thode had several outbursts, inappropriate participation, and disobeyed warning letters during the course of the class. The plaintiff's father, Stephen Thode, who is a longtime professor of finance at Lehigh, testified to his daughter's scores being irregular. He also said no student of Lehigh ever scored zero for a course after attending and participating in every class.

17

MAN SUES HIMSELF

Believe it or not, there are a couple of cases where people have sued themselves. In 1976, Peter Maxwell was severely injured when his sweater caught on the bolt of a machine. Although it is not uncommon to sue a workplace when injuries such as this occur, what was odd was that Maxwell owned the company. Although Maxwell owned 95% of the company, the other 5% was owned by another couple, and this only permitted him to give himself a limited salary each year. Despite partial ownership of the company, he was not at liberty to increase his salary because he was still an employee—hence taking the issue to court. Maxwell sought and won compensation both to aid with his medical bills as well as lost wages incurred from his injuries.

18

HIGH SCHOOL STUDENT CAUGHT SLEEPING

Even if you've never fallen asleep in a class, you have most likely fallen asleep somewhere you shouldn't have at one time or another. This strange lawsuit occurred when a 16-year-old high school student at Danbury High School in Connecticut claimed a teacher woke them in a rude manner that resulted in permanent damages. Vinicios Robacher reported that his teacher smacked his desk hard enough to cause hearing loss.

The plaintiff's father, Soel Robacher, planned to sue the Connecticut Board of Education, Danbury High School, and the city on behalf of his child. His father claimed that the teacher smacking the desk caused his son's eardrum to burst because the boy was resting his left ear on the desk. He further stated that Vinicios experienced nearly complete hearing loss.

Since the beginning of the case, the family claimed that their son had gone through extensive medical care and would require surgery, and only some of his hearing was restored with the help of an ear, nose, and throat specialist. In addition to medical issues, their son was teased by classmates — enough that they needed to transfer him to a private school. Unlike some of the other cases in this book, there are still many pending aspects to the lawsuit.

The attorney, Alan Barry, reported that there were many circumstances that required investigation before any decisions were made on the case. First off, a full medical analysis of the teen's current condition and an investigation into the teacher is required regarding the instructor's history and methods to determine their character. Aside from the hearing loss, the student claims to have suffered emotional damage.

19

TOO HOT TO HANDLE

The McDonald's hot coffee case is another infamous lawsuit that gained international attention. In 1994, 79-year-old Stella Liebeck filed a claim against McDonald's. She ordered a 49-cent coffee at a McDonald's drive-through window in Albuquerque,

New Mexico. The woman rode in the passenger seat while her grandson drove, and since the car didn't have a cup holder, they had to park to add cream and sugar to the coffee. In the process of opening the lid, the beverage spilled into Liebeck's lap. The coffee was hot enough to scar her groin, buttocks, and thighs.

Upon arriving at the hospital, it was determined that Liebeck had incurred third-degree burns on 6% of her skin. There were other lesser burns covering 60% of other skin areas. Liebeck was hospitalized for eight days and underwent a skin graft during the stay. In those eight days, Liebeck lost weight (9.1kg) and had to spend an extra three weeks at home, cared for by her daughter. She was left with a partial disability for two years and a permanent disfigurement.

The lawsuit was filed after Liebeck tried settling with McDonald's for $20,000 for the expenses she paid, but the fast-food chain offered her $800. With their refusal to raise the offer, Liebeck's Texas attorney, Reed Morgan, filed a lawsuit. The suit accused the company of negligence and selling unreasonably dangerous coffee. Morgan requested $90,000, which McDonald's refused. Later, before the trial, other mediators offered $225,000, but Morgan asked for $300,000, and McDonald's refused both.

During the trial, Liebeck's attorney said McDonald's coffee is served at 180–190°F, and that temperature can cause a third-degree burn within 12–15 seconds of contact to the skin. The attorneys also told the court that other coffee franchises serve theirs at a lower temperature that would allow you to clean spilled coffee without causing any harm to the skin. McDonald's, in their defense, said the coffee temperature is higher because most of their customers are commuters and have a long way to drive, so they aim to keep the coffee hot throughout the trip.

The court verdict found McDonald's to be 80% responsible for the burns and Liebeck 20% at fault. Although the jury noted that there was a warning on the cup, it wasn't bold enough. The jury awarded Liebeck $200,000 in compensation for damages but reduced it to $160,000 (because it was 20% her fault). She was also awarded $2.7 million in punitive damages, which was later reduced to $900,000. Both McDonalds and Liebeck appealed the case, and both parties settled out of court with an undisclosed settlement. Liebeck died at age 91, and her daughter said the years following the court case took a toll on her mother. Everything was a result of the burns and the court proceedings, she said. She also said the settlement they got from McDonald's was used to pay for a live-in nurse.

20

THE CASE OF THE MISSING GAS

Some lawsuits will leave you wondering whether they are a joke. One example is that of a Michigan woman seeking $5 million because her repossessed car was returned with a missing $29.44 worth of gas. When Victoria Jean Church-Dellinger defaulted on the payments for her leased car, her lender, Ally Financial Inc., had the vehicle repossessed. When the vehicle was repossessed, only a half-tank of the gasoline that Church-Dellinger had purchased remained. The plaintiff provided photos of the fuel gauge, gas receipt, odometer reading, and other evidence to prove her accusations.

Church-Dellinger's repossessed car was a 2008 Pontiac G6, and it has a capacity of 16 gallons. Each gallon at the time of the case in Michigan was running at $3.68. Church-Dellinger alleged that she had about 8 gallons of gas sitting in the car which amounted to a total of $29.44 worth in the Pontiac. The lawsuit was based on the argument that, after repossessing a car, all personal properties of the owner must be returned, including the gasoline.

21

FOR THE LOVE OF BUTTER

Imagine being awarded a whopping $7.2 million from a lawsuit. This was the exact amount a man named Wayne Watson received when he won his case against three food companies. The companies were The Kroger Co., Gilster-Mary Lee Corp., and Dillon Companies Inc. Watson developed a respiratory problem in 2007, which the lawsuit claimed was caused by constant inhalation of their microwave popcorn's artificial butter. Watson was diagnosed with "popcorn lung," a disease formerly known as bronchiolitis obliterans. Diacetyl is a chemical found in popcorn flavoring, and it is strongly associated with the illness that Watson contracted.

"Popcorn lung" has been documented for decades as a disease mostly contracted among factory workers. Watson is the first ever case reported to develop the illness as a result of consuming popcorn. Watson's love for the snack made him consume it every night, often eating two bags or more. He also enjoyed inhaling the steam of the newly opened bag of the said snack, which supposedly contributed to the development of "popcorn lung."

A series of tests were carried out in Watson's home, and the results revealed that there were significant peak levels of the chemical diacetyl, matching the levels found in factories. The lawsuit stated that neither the manufacturers nor supermarket retail outlets had warning labels for consumers who inhaled the buttery aroma. Also, the smell was appealing, and no consumer would think it could pose the risk of developing an illness, especially not a serious lung-related illness. Watson went on to win the case and was awarded $7.2 million.

22

NOT REAL TUNA

Subway's sandwich shops are well-known giants in the fast-food industry. A case was filed against the sandwich franchise by Nilima Amin in California in 2022. She accused the company of misleading her and other consumers into believing their product contained 100% tuna, which was not true. The restaurant chain requested the case be dismissed, but the judge refused and said the lawsuit should move forward.

The lawsuit was cited after a biologist analyzed 20 samples of the Subway sandwich and found no trace of tuna DNA sequence in 19 of the samples. The lawsuit further stated that the 20 samples were pulled from 20 different branches of the restaurant chain and proved there was no way it was a mistake. Furthermore, the biologist saw other animal DNA in the sample, including that of pork and chicken.

Subway, in their defense, said their sandwich contains other ingredients like mayonnaise, which contains eggs. The company still insisted they used 100% wild-caught tuna in their sandwich.

The plaintiff sought a jury trial and a class-action status accusing the restaurant of unfair competition, false advertising, and fraud. The lawsuit sought restitution and punitive damages. The Subway spokesperson insisted on the company's integrity and use of 100% tuna fish. The suit maintained that no customer ordering Subway's sandwich should be given a sandwich containing other animal or miscellaneous products because the company stated they offer a 100% tuna sandwich. After months of the lawsuit, *The New York Times* also obtained samples from different Subway locations for testing. They found no DNA of tuna species in all the samples tested. Through those months, Subway stood its ground that they use wild-caught skipjack tuna and are regulated by the Food and Drug Administration. The company said all the DNA tests carried out were done with unreliable DNA testing that cannot determine the contents of a food sample, especially when processed and cooked. The judge gave Subway a partial victory.

23

NOT THE PRICE
THEY CRAVED

A New Jersey couple, Nelson Estrella-Rojas and his wife Joann Estrella, sued both Taco Bell and its parent company, Yum! Brands for overcharging them for two Chalupa Cravings Boxes. The cravings boxes were advertised for $5, but the franchise charged $12.18 for two boxes. They charged a total of $12.99, which included the 81-cent state sales tax. This was what made the couple question the management for charging them $12.18 for what should have been $10 ($5 for each box) plus tax.

Taco Bell, in their defense, said that the TV commercial had a clear disclaimer stating: "price may vary." The promo price was only valid at a particular location for a specific period which had a limit. Even with that, the couple claimed the disclaimer should have been in a type and size that was clear and relative to other type sizes of the advert. The lawsuit also noted that the disclaimer lasted for only 3 seconds while the advert lasted 30 seconds.

The couple was asking for compensation for time wasted driving to Taco Bell, gasoline expenses, and $2.18 (the difference between what was charged by Taco Bell before tax and what they thought was the expected cost). The suit also accused Taco Bell of attempting to attract a larger market sale and increase profits with its false advertisement. The couple asked for compensation, punitive damages, and court and attorney fees.

Taco Bell's lawyer, Allen Burton, filed a motion to move the case to the federal court from the superior court in Middlesex Borough, New Jersey, which was successful. The lawyer's reason was that both Taco Bell and Yum! have their headquarters in New Jersey.

24

A NOT SO HAPPY ENDING

The McDonald's Happy Meal made its debut in 1979 and since then has been a staple on the menu. A Quebec father, Antonio Bramante, filed a class-action lawsuit against the franchise, accusing McDonald's of breaking provincial law against advertising to children under 13 years of age. Mr. Bramante claimed that McDonald's targeting of children led him to have to eat at the franchise at least once a week due to his kids' insistence. He is estimated to have spent hundreds of dollars for his children on Happy Meals, which entice youth with their toys from popular films. The lawsuit sought compensation, punitive damages, and discontinuation of the practice by McDonald's in the province. Bramante won an unknown amount in a settlement with McDonald's.

25

A STOLEN SLOGAN

In 2015, Vegadelphia Food sued Beyond Meat and Dunkin' for trademark infringement. Since 2013, Vegadelphia Food has used the slogan "Where Great Taste is Plant-Based," for which they received a federal trademark in 2015.

The complaint was filed in U.S. District Court in Florida. Vegadelphia also accused Dunkin' of replicating some of its imagery and branding. Some of the similar branding ideas that Dunkin' used include their sun background, text, and font size, and the food corporation believed it was more than just a mere coincidence. Snoop Dogg was involved in the TV commercial, and the filing made mention of the star's first line, handing a customer a sandwich and saying, "You want that Plant-Based Great Taste fresh out of the oven?"

The United States Patent and Trademark Office said there is a likelihood of confusion between Vegadelphia and Dunkin' trademarks. Vegadelphia, in the suit, stated that Dunkin's sandwich generated a revenue of over $135 million within six months of sales with an estimated profit margin of 60%. In the suit, Vegadelphia asked Dunkin' for a royalty of an equitable portion for infringement of property, punitive damages, statutory damages, attorney fees, and costs.

26

A FRUITLESS LAWSUIT

In 2016, a class action lawsuit was filed against Krispy Kreme's claims of using "natural ingredients" in their maple, blueberry, and raspberry products. The law firm Faruqi & Faruqi represented

Jason Saidian in California, accusing Krispy Kreme of misleading their customers. The donut ingredients included sugar, artificial coloring, and corn syrup, but the donuts were represented as if they contained authentic, natural ingredients. When investigated, it was discovered that the maple products did not contain maple sugar or syrup, and the fruit products did not contain any real fruit. The plaintiff said that if he had known this, he would not have paid such a high price for the treats. Jason Saidian requested the company pay over $5 million in damages and stop falsely advertising natural ingredients in their products.

27

A FREAKY AMOUNT
OF COLLISIONS

Jimmy John's motto is "Freaky Fresh! Freaky Fast!" and has landed the franchise's name in quite a few lawsuits involving reckless driving. In all the cases, the plaintiffs accused Jimmy John's of failing to train their drivers properly. The franchise's policies were under attack as the limited delivery time pressured drivers to drive as fast as possible and created an environment that encouraged reckless driving.

In August of 2017, Connie Sue Brown and her daughter, Karen, were in a car accident involving a Jimmy John's delivery driver, Eli Beam. Beam struck the back end of the Browns' car at an intersection in Glen Carbon, Illinois. Connie Sue Brown continued with a lawsuit against both Eli Beam and the Jimmy John's franchise for $50,000 in compensation for the pain, suffering, discomfort, lost wages, and medical expenses incurred from injuries caused during the accident.

This was not the only record of Jimmy John's motto coming under scrutiny. In 2011, a Jimmy John's delivery driver cut in front of a 19-year-old motorcyclist, ending in a catastrophic accident. Ty Cirillo was on his way to work at Aria in Las Vegas when the delivery driver took a sharp left turn into Cirillo's path. The 19-year-old man's pelvis was damaged, and he suffered many broken limbs, ultimately needing both hips replaced and requiring the use of a wheelchair for the rest of his life. The young man would never work or walk again. This led Cirillo to take the franchise to court, attacking Jimmy John's motto, training practices, and lack of repercussions for their drivers violating traffic laws.

Although this was a multi-million-dollar lawsuit seeking compensation for the life cruelly robbed from Cirillo, it also served the higher purpose of attempting to make changes in the corporation's structure to help protect future motorists from being injured for the sake of speedy sandwich delivery.

In 2010, Bob Reynolds was riding his motorcycle through Springfield, Illinois, when he was struck by a Jimmy John's driver. The accident resulted in injuries severe enough to require seven surgeries for the 64-year-old man. Reynolds's case accused Jimmy John's 15-minute delivery policy of being the culprit for accidents such as these. The franchise's lawyer argued that it is not the responsibility of the employer to train a driver who had claimed experience prior to being hired and, therefore, should already understand they are expected to avoid unnecessary dangers while out on deliveries. Reynolds had received $100,000 from the driver's insurance company, but the medical bills from his multiple surgeries amounted to much more than the money received, which is what he hoped the lawsuit would cover.

All these cases are overshadowed by one of the worst. In February 2014, Linda Lutman filed a lawsuit against Jimmy John's on behalf of her father,

J. Robert McClain. The previous August, 79-year-old McClain was walking his dog when he was struck by a Jimmy John's manager completing a delivery. The investigation determined that the driver was looking at his clock when he failed to see McClain and ran into him. J. Robert McClain left behind his loving wife, daughter, and grandchildren, and the family sought compensation not only for the loss of income but for the loss of companionship his wife suffered during their retirement years.

In these cases, Jimmy John's speedy delivery policies came under attack, and in all of them, the franchise argued they were not at fault. To this day, the restaurant chain still uses the same "Freaky Fresh! Freaky Fast!" Although some of the cases against Jimmy John's won out, many of them are still wrapped up in litigation.

28

SHORTER THAN EXPECTED

Subway sandwiches made a name for themselves with its healthier menu options and hallmark foot-long sandwiches. In January 2013, Australian resident Matt Corby posted an image on social media proving that his "foot-long" sub fell short by an inch. DeNittis, Osefchen, and Zimmerman Law Offices seized the opportunity to take Subway to court, representing ten plaintiffs in a case against the sandwich shop franchise. As part of the case, many loaves of the restaurant's sandwich bread were measured, and although many of them met the advertised 12 inches, enough of them measured a quarter inch too short that the case ended in a settlement. Even though each plaintiff was only awarded $5,000, this amounted to a whopping half a million dollars in total in this lawsuit.

29

NOT THE ONLY ONE

In 2020, Budweiser's company Anheuser-Busch released its certified-organic Michelob Ultra Hard Seltzer. The advertisement campaign claimed that it was the only company producing an organic hard seltzer, which sent Suzie's Brewery to court against them. Although Suzie's Brewery, an Oregon-based producer of craft beer, sold organic hard seltzers in fewer states than Anheuser-Busch, their product was on the market before Busch's. With a smaller marketing budget, Suzie's Brewery suffered as a result of Anheuser-Busch's marketing campaigns, which made health-conscious consumers believe that there was only one hard seltzer option available—a tactic known in the industry as the "bully-pulpit" method. As such, Suzie's Brewery filed a claim. Although no money resulted from this lawsuit, Anheuser-Busch received a restraining order, forcing them to suspend further airing of the commercial, claiming they provided a wholly unique product.

30

CAN'T GET ENOUGH

In 2016, Angela Ebner took Fresh, Inc., to court over a $24.00 Sugar Lip Treatment. This frivolous case claimed that the company was misleading its customers on account of the "screw-up" styled packaging that stopped dispensing the lip scrub with 25% of the product going unused.

The court ruled that the company did not violate any state or federal laws because all the products' labels were accurate. The weight of the product and the quantity of balm in it were clearly labeled. The court also said any user who wasn't satisfied with its dispensing function could use a little tool or their finger to scrape out the remaining lip balm when the tube stopped working. For all those reasons, the court dismissed the case. In other words, Ebner ended up with the cost of lawyer fees on top of her $24.00 luxury lip balm.

31

A CONSPIRACY ON ICE

In 2016, Stace Pincus of Illinois filed a $5 million lawsuit against Starbucks on account of the amount of ice they put in their iced coffees. The argument was that the coffee company was intentionally deceiving customers into paying full price for half of the product by filling half of the cup with ice. Starbucks counter-debated that customers are purchasing the cup size, not the product volume itself. When they purchase a 24-ounce coffee, they are asking for a 24-ounce cup, not necessarily 24 ounces of beverage.

This was not an isolated instance of someone heading to court over their Starbucks iced coffee. That same year, Alexander Forouzesh of California pressed another case against Starbucks with the same claims — that Starbucks was intentionally swindling customers by filling cold cups with more ice than coffee. The judge ended up dismissing the case and made two valid points: first, that the cups were clear and, therefore, any reasonable customer is not deceived, as they can clearly see how much ice is added to the cup. Second, Starbucks allows customers to order their iced coffees without ice if they wish. True, it is just a cold coffee at that point, but the option is there to receive the full 24 ounces if the customer so desires.

32

SLACKING
ON THE FILLING

A Columbia, Missouri, man named Robert Bratton filed a class action lawsuit alleging Reese's had too much slack-fill in their products. Bratton made this discovery after he purchased several boxes of Reese's Pieces and Whoppers for $1 per box. He argued that the containers were opaque; therefore, he was misled into believing there was more candy inside than there actually was. The candy company, The Hershey Company, moved the case to a federal high court from the state court where it was initially filed. The company further motioned for the judge to throw out the case, but the court denied their request.

The candy company was charged under a 50-year-old law of the Missouri Merchandising Practice Act (MMPA) which aims at protecting customers against unfair practices by business owners. In her ruling, U.S. District Judge Nanette Laughrey stated that Bratton accused the company that their packaging was deceiving. She further said those claims were enough reason to file an allegation under the MMPA for unlawful practice. Laughrey said the candy boxes clearly stated their net weight and number of pieces in each package, but Bratton continued to argue that about 29% of the box was air and he would not have purchased the candy if he had known this. With this in mind, Bratton regularly purchased these boxes of candy, despite the slack-fill, for years before taking the candy company to court.

33

BACHELOR PARTY
GONE WRONG

In 1996, 38-year-old Florida resident Paul Shimkonis attended his bachelor party at the Diamond Doll Club the night before his wedding. Although this is not an uncommon way to celebrate a "stag party," this particular night took an odd turn of events. During the party, Shimkonis supposedly received whiplash from a stripper named Tawny Peaks.

Shimkonis filed a lawsuit claiming to have suffered severe bodily injuries, pain, disability, mental anguish, disfigurement, loss of concentration, and the will to enjoy life, among many other sufferings. He sustained all those injuries when the stripper forcefully tucked his face into her 60-inch bust. Shimkonis said, as funny as other people might find it, it was no joke to him. He claimed that the stripper also slammed her breasts on his head, which almost knocked him out. He described the incident as two bricks hitting him simultaneously. "I've never been right since then," he said. When asked why he did not receive immediate medical attention, the Florida man stated he took two months to see a doctor due to the humiliation caused by the incident.

Shimkonis, who was a physical therapist, sought $15,000 from Peaks (the stripper) and Diamond Dolls Club, where the incident happened, for the damages he incurred. In a statement, the club manager said that if he were in Shimkonis's shoes, he would have loved what the stripper did, and no one would hear him complain.

34

VIDEO GAME VIOLENCE LEADS TO TRAGEDY

April 20, 1999, is a day the Columbine High School students and staff will forever remember. It was the day the Colorado school experienced a tragic shooting and an attempted bombing. Tragically, two 12th-grade students, Eric Harris and Dylan Klebold, killed 15 of their classmates. The shootout between the students and the police ended with 21 others severely injured. This tragic event is among the deadliest high school shootings in U.S. history.

The family of the slain teacher, Dave Sanders, filed a lawsuit representing the victims. The case stated that the shooters were influenced by violent video games. Some of the violent video game makers mentioned in the suit include Time Warner Inc., Palm Pictures, Activision, Sony Computer Entertainment America, and id software. U.S. District Judge Lewis Babcock granted a motion to dismiss the lawsuit against Time Warner Inc. and Palm Pictures. During the ruling, Judge Babcock said no violent game maker or movie could have foreseen that their product would cause the Columbine shooting or any violence. However, during the investigation, police found a videotape showing one of the killers with a gun which he called "Arlene." Arlene was a character in a violent video game. The plaintiff also claimed that the shooters had watched *The Basketball Diaries*, a movie in which a student killed his fellow classmates. Although this is not the only civil lawsuit brought against media for violent images and storylines marketed to youth, to this day, no media companies have taken responsibility for their possible roles in tragedies such as the Columbine shooting.

35

A NOVEL IDEA

When someone steals your trade secret, you have the right to sue them. This was the case for Charles Joyce and James Voigt. The duo lived in Wisconsin and filed a lawsuit against PepsiCo and their distribution partners, Wis-Pak Inc. and Carolina Canners Inc. Joyce and Voigt told the press that they had worked hard to come up with the idea of selling purified water in an individual serving.

In their lawsuit, the plaintiffs stated that PepsiCo was using their trade secret. PepsiCo didn't respond to the case; therefore, the court granted the duo the sum of $1.26 million based on the revenue the company had generated at the time of filing the case regarding the product. PepsiCo, in their defense, said the accusations were dubious and that they weren't aware of the lawsuit until after the court granted the award to the plaintiff.

PepsiCo said they deserved a trial before such judgment could be made. They requested the court toss out the ruling and give them a chance to challenge the accusations. The company claimed that the lawsuit was served to them in North Carolina instead of their New York base, which is why the secretary failed to act on the letters sent. A PepsiCo spokesperson stated that the company wanted a chance to dispute the claims. He further said the lack of response was a result of "internal process issues," and when given an opportunity to defend the allegation, they wanted the chance to make a case rather than proceeding with the payout.

The plaintiffs claimed to have had a written confidentiality agreement with Wis-Park and Carolina Canners (PepsiCo distributors in Wisconsin) in 1981. About 15 years later, the companies gave their idea to PepsiCo, which PepsiCo used in developing their Aquafina water products. There was no proof that the plaintiffs patented their concept; it might not stand as a strong claim that the idea was theirs. PepsiCo, in their defense, said they knew nothing about any agreement between Joyce and Voigt and their distributor partners.

NO FRUIT
IN THE LOOPS

Froot Loops by Kellogg's is a familiar cereal brand, most popular among children for its sweet taste, colorful marketing, and fun toucan mascot. The cereal was originally released in 1959 with the name Fruit Loops. The Paxton v. Kellogg's lawsuit caused the name change to Froot Loops. Despite this change, the company still faced another lawsuit regarding its name and was asked to pay damages of $5 million for misleading customers into thinking that there was actual fruit in their product. The lawsuit attacked the company for selling Froot Loops cereal with bright pictures that resemble fruits, leading consumers to believe there is actual fruit within the cereal. The plaintiff had once filed a similar case but was rejected by a federal judge twice. The judge stated that the word "Froot" and the ring shape of the cereal doesn't reasonably imply ingredients as real fruits. In the end, this third case was dismissed on a technicality as Kellogg's had not been served properly.

37

NOT ENOUGH TIME

The instructions on food packaging are meant to guide consumers on how to prepare it. Customers expect these instructions and cooking times to be correct when they purchase boxed meals. This led Amanda Ramirez to file a suit against Kraft Heinz Food Company. She proposed a $5 million lawsuit claiming that their Velveeta Shells & Cheese takes a longer time to cook than what was stated on the packaging. The instructions for cooking the pasta claimed that it was microwaveable and required just 3½ minutes to be ready for consumption.

The plaintiff's attorney said the pasta requires four minutes to prepare. The food company, in a statement, referred to the allegations as frivolous and said they were ready to defend their product.

In the suit, Ramirez's lawyers said the company was profiting from the false advertisement of the product because they knew customers trusted the brand to be honest. They further noted that the product was sold at a premium price with their misleading marketing promise that the product could be ready in 3½ minutes which quickly catches any customer's attention, enticing the purchase of this product over another. Aside from the $5 million, the plaintiff requested punitive damages and for the company to cease the deceptive advertisement and engage in corrective advertising practices and campaigns.

38

THE HOTEL
SLIPPED UP

An Orange County man, William Anthony Packard, demanded between $200,000 and $1 million in settlement for an injury he sustained at Hilton Houston Downtown. Packard was said to have slipped and fallen on lettuce leaves thrown on the floor of the hotel's banquet area. He claimed to have suffered injuries to his right hip, left knee, one elbow, back, and both his ankles as a result of the fall. He further claimed he was traumatized by the fall.

The plaintiff was reported to have visited the hotel to attend a private event during which he was hosting about 40 important guests. The dinner for the event was scheduled to begin at 6:30 p.m., and the hotel's staff took a long time to serve the main course.

Packard stood up from his table to inquire about the delay, which was when he slipped on the lettuce and fell on the hotel's marble floor.

The lawsuit accused American Liberty Hospitality (the company managing the hotel) of failure to address customer safety, negligence, and lack of supervision. He said the hotel did not have enough staff to handle the special guests' needs. He argued that if there had been enough staff on board, their meal wouldn't have been delayed, and he wouldn't have ended up slipping in the first place.

39

NOT AUTHENTICALLY TEXAN

Texas Pete, a hot sauce made by TW Garner Food Co., turned out not to be as Texan as some customers believed. The majority of consumers believed the hot sauce to be a product of the Lone Star State (Texas). However, the condiment originated in North Carolina in 1929 at a barbeque restaurant. Philip White, a California man, sued the company with an argument that their branding was misleading customers to believe the product was Texan and therefore garnering customer loyalty under false pretenses.

The plaintiff purchased the condiment for $3 in a grocery store in Los Angeles. The product contained a label featuring a cowboy, which became part of White's argument as the cowboy is a common symbolic image associated with the Texan lifestyle. White said he purchased the product with the influence of the image displayed on the product label. Afterward, he realized that not only was it a North Carolina product, but the recipe was Louisiana-inspired instead of Texas-inspired. The plaintiff said if he had known the sauce wasn't made in Texas; he wouldn't have purchased it. He further said the company was using the name to cheat its way to generate market leads worth billions.

Texas Pete, in a statement, explained how the name came about. The founder, Garner, and his son sought the expertise of a marketing advisor, and they came up with "Mexican Joe" to be the initial name. But Garner and his son thought their product needed an American name. Texas was known for its reputation for spicy cuisine, so Garner named the product Texas Pete (Pete was his son's nickname).

40

HUGGED TOO TIGHT

The act of hugging is one form of physical touch that can convey different meanings, such as love, emotional security, romance, intimacy, or friendship. Unfortunately, this was not the kind of hug a woman working in China experienced from her colleagues.

Although her name is kept private, the case took place in the Yunxi Court in 2021. The Chinese woman reported that a coworker approached her and gave her an extremely tight hug. The hug caused her enough pain to make her scream. After the hug, she reported experiencing pain throughout the workday. She tried using several home remedies, thinking it was a minor discomfort. After the pain persisted for days, she decided to visit a hospital to get medical help. She was recommended to take an X-ray, which showed that three of her ribs were broken (two on the right side and one on the left).

A year after the incident happened, the woman filed a case against the coworker. The suit alleged that the incident forced her to take a leave of absence from work, which later cost her the job. She also said the incident caused her a financial burden because she had to settle the hospital bills. The man, in his defense, said the woman's allegations were false, and there was no evidence that his friendly hug brought about her injury. After the court hearing, the judge ordered the man to give his coworker (the woman) 10,000 Yuan in damages (about $1,500).

41

TOO MUCH BOOZE

For a beer to be labeled "non-alcoholic," it must contain less than 0.5% alcohol per volume (ABV), while the label "alcohol-free" brew must indicate 0% ABV. In 2019, Louisiana resident Kathleen M. Wilson sued Heineken under the pretense that their non-alcoholic beer, Heineken 0.0, contained too much alcohol. The label listed the beverage as "alcohol-free." Wilson argued that the product's label was misleading because it contained 0.3% alcohol and that most customers looking for this kind of beverage are looking to replicate the taste of alcoholic beverages without consuming any. The plaintiff said that every consumer deserves to know the ingredients (alcohol content and percentage included) in the product they are consuming.

Heineken addressed the issue on their website, pointing out that the fermentation of the product was natural, so a minuscule percentage of alcohol could be found. The statement further explained that 0.3 percent ABV was much lower when compared with other products that have a natural fermentation process. They also said all their product labels were correct and in line with federal regulations and requirements for an alcohol-free beverage.

The plaintiff complained that if she had known the product had 0.3% alcohol, she wouldn't have purchased it. She said Heineken portraying their product as alcohol-free was false and deceptive, and she had suffered damages. She asked for injunctive relief that Heineken change the labeling on the product, monetary damages, and court costs.

42

A MARRIAGE RUINED

Uber, a popular transportation company, has made a name for itself as a ride-share service. The company was made famous for its drivers picking up customers in their private vehicles and getting them to their destinations through the means of the Uber app. Though many people have decent experiences with this service, a French man, whose identity remains private, sued the company, blaming it for ending his marriage.

The plaintiff claimed that there was a bug in the app that provided his wife with information about his whereabouts and places he had been. He said he logged into his Uber app on his wife's iPhone and was sure that he logged off after using it. However, he claimed that his wife (now ex-wife) kept receiving notifications (his take-offs and drop-offs) on her phone. In the lawsuit, the man requested the company pay €45 million ($48 million) for the damages and pain they caused him. The main concern brought up in the lawsuit was not about emotional distress but about privacy. Other users have reported that even after logging out of the app, the phone may still receive notifications updating outside parties about the account user's whereabouts, which could put users at risk.

43

DON'T FALL
OFF THE DONKEY

A 58-year-old lady, Kimberly Bonn, accused the Mexican restaurant El Jalisco in Tallahassee of negligence. It is a common practice for customers to climb a life-size donkey statue for a photo opportunity when they visit the restaurant. Unfortunately, when Bonn attempted to do this in August 2015, she fell and fractured her spine, which resulted in her becoming bedridden for 18 months. She took the restaurant to court, asking for damages worth more than $15,000. She accused the restaurant of encouraging patrons to ride the donkey statue without providing safety features like a ladder or non-slip saddle. Bonn also described the donkey statue to be too smooth and slick not to have protective features.

The lawsuit resulted in a social media hashtag war. Tallahassee residents split into two campaigns, with some avid El Jalisco patrons taking proud pictures in the franchise and using the hashtag #ForTheDonkey, while supporters of Bonn's case responded with the hashtag #ForThePeople. In the end, the lawsuit was dropped, and the restaurant's attorneys responded to Bonn's claims by stating she understood the risks when she decided to mount the donkey statue for a photograph.

44

THE TEENAGE TAKEAWAY

It is not uncommon for parents to take their children's phones away for all kinds of reasons, whether it is to promote general wellness, encourage a focus on schoolwork, or even as a punishment. Most teenagers have experienced getting into trouble and having their phones taken away. Despite how common this is, a 15-year-old teenager decided to file a lawsuit against his mother after his phone was taken away in hopes that it would help him study. He argued that his mother mistreated him by taking away his phone, but the judge failed to buy the argument. The judge said it was natural for every parent to take some steps to ensure their kids improved their schoolwork. The judge sided with the mother and said he believed she took the right action, just like every responsible parent would. He further said if she had allowed her son to get distracted from studying by his mobile phone, she would be irresponsible. Despite the absurdity of this lawsuit, it is not the only one of its kind in which a teen has taken their parent to court over technology restrictions.

45

A PAINFUL EXPERIENCE

A Texas resident named Jennifer Lindahl filed a lawsuit against the U.S. government over burns she received from nacho cheese. The incident took place at Sheppard Air Force Base when one of the employees accidentally spilled hot cheese on her hand. Lindahl took the issue to court, requesting $95,000 for court costs, hospital bills, and to cover other damages incurred from the accident.

When the cheese was spilled on Lindahl's hand, another attendant immediately attempted to help by wiping the cheese away with a rag. However, the burn was bad enough that the upper layer of the woman's skin peeled off with the cheese. The lawsuit claimed that the U.S. government was careless, negligent, and reckless.

The argument proceeded to list that the nacho cheese was heated to an inappropriately high temperature and the employees were not well-trained, which resulted in the spill, and that the attendant who wiped the cheese away created further damage.

In the suit, the plaintiff claimed to have sought treatment at the United Regional Health Care System emergency room. The wound was cleaned, treated, and bandaged with no pain medication. The injury, instead of healing, got worse, and she had more trips to a doctor. After follow-up appointments, Lindahl was informed that the injury was serious enough to require surgery. This restricted her from using her hand, which eventually caused her to lose her job.

46

FIRST DATE
FAILURE

Taking a date to the movies is a popular choice for many people and is often a pleasant experience. Unfortunately, this was not the case for Texas resident Brendan Vezmar. Vezmar decided to take a date to watch *Guardians of the Galaxy, Vol. 2* and found himself disappointed when the woman texted throughout the movie. He asked her to stop multiple times and reported that she continued to text every 10–20 minutes. This was the reason he decided to take her to court in hopes of receiving the $17.31 that he had spent on her movie ticket. The CEO of the movie theater offered to pay for the ticket; however, Vezmar wanted his date to pay the price. She refused to cover the cost of her movie ticket. In court, Vezmar stated that she affected his viewing experience and, therefore, she should be the one to re-pay him. In the end, she apologized, agreed to pay for the cost of the movie, and requested Vezmar never contact her again.

47

A TRAUMATIC INVESTIGATION

In October 2014, a 56-year-old man from Florida named John Timiriasieff had his right leg amputated at Doctors Hospital in Coral Gables. After the amputation, Timiriasieff was visited by detectives who found his leg discarded in a waste facility, still attached to a tag with his name on it. This is what led him to take the facility to court for the emotional distress caused by the incident.

According to Florida law, there is a proper way to dispose of amputated body parts, which includes incinerating the remains. However, Doctors Hospital simply threw the plaintiff's amputated limb into the garbage with his personal information still attached. Aside from Timiriasieff having to undergo questioning by detectives during his recovery, his medical information was not protected by the hospital. Although the amount requested was not released, Timiriasieff asked for monetary compensation.

48

NO WAY OFF

Jose Martinez took a ride on Disney's "It's a Small World" in 2009 and ended up getting stuck for over 30 minutes. The disabled man claimed that he was the only passenger not evacuated from the ride when it broke down, and due to being paralyzed, he was unable to leave on his own. Furthermore, the entire time the incident occurred, the song "It's a Small World" continued playing on repeat, which added to the trauma of the event. In addition to needing a wheelchair, Martinez was subject to panic attacks and high blood pressure, which were aggravated by the conditions.

The lawsuit accused Disneyland staff of negligence, as he was the only person who was not properly evacuated while the ride was repaired. Martinez was unable to receive any form of attention until after the ride was fixed, which was when he was taken to the first aid station. At this point, it took over three hours for the medical staff to stabilize him, and he was terrified enough to urinate on himself while trapped on the ride. Martinez was awarded $8,000 for his pain and suffering and for violation of the disability law.

49

THE PIGGY BANK INCIDENT

Idaho residents Lonnie and Karen Boozer were on a family trip to Disneyland with their children when they stopped at the Space Trade gift shop to purchase gifts for their young daughters. Thereafter, the couple was accused of stealing a piggy bank and was detained by Disneyland security for questioning. While at the security office, the couple's two-year-old daughter was terrified when she witnessed two staff members remove the heads of their costumes and hold them in their arms.

The couple decided to press a lawsuit against Disney, asking for $1 million on account of false accusations and attempted imprisonment. Aside from the shoplifting accusations, the couple reported that their daughter was emotionally traumatized following the incident with the "headless" characters, reporting that she became depressed following the experience. The little girl ended up needing three months of therapy to deal with the shock of seeing the "dismembered" costumes. The lawsuit settled for an undisclosed amount.

50

AFRAID OF THE
SMALL THINGS

Maria C. Waltherr-Willard taught and served the Mariemont School District as a high school French and Spanish teacher for 35 years. Throughout her time working with teenagers, she sought therapy and was diagnosed with multiple phobias, which included a phobia of small children. She was also diagnosed with anxiety and hypertension. Normally, this did not affect her ability to work. However, in 2009, Ohio High School eliminated its French program, and the school transferred Waltherr-Willard to teach a Spanish program for younger students. They did this despite knowing her phobia and medical diagnosis.

Waltherr-Willard took the school district to court for discrimination and sought compensation for not only past emotional damages but future ones, as well as her attorney fees. The plaintiff argued that she presented her medical documentation to the school district when she requested a transfer back to the high school, which was denied. In court, she drew attention to her severe anxiety and made it clear that it caused her blood pressure to rise enough to put her at risk of having a stroke if she was forced to work under such conditions. She also claimed that the school district held a contract with her, exempting her from teaching younger students, which did not hold up in court.

51

FAILED TO DEPLOY

In 2012, Tammy and John Haines purchased a Jeep Grand Cherokee Laredo from a Chrysler dealer in West Virginia. During a medical emergency, Tammy ended up in an accident where she ran into another vehicle as well as two utility poles. During the accident, the airbags failed to work, and the fuel pump did not turn off, which led her to take the dealership to court. Haines requested $75,000 for negligence and breach of contract. The woman also claimed that the injuries she sustained were worsened by the failure of the vehicle's safety features.

52

A RUDE ENCOUNTER

Joel Acey took his child to eat at a Bob Evans franchise in December of 2010. According to Acey, he asked the hostess to seat him at the front of the restaurant, where there was plenty of open seating. Instead of sitting him there, she placed him at the back of the restaurant and even went as far as to call him an idiot while seating him. The waitress apologized on behalf of the hostess after hearing what she said to him. The manager was called to the table, and Acey was offered a free meal, which he declined.

Despite the attempt at immediate reparations made by the restaurant's staff, Joel Acey still took the situation to court, seeking compensation and punitive damages as he believed the hostility was a result of racial discrimination. After going through with the lawsuit, Acey even received threats from anonymous phone numbers, all of which reported to the restaurant's parent company, Bob Evans Farms, Inc.

53

KICKED FROM THE TEAM

It is a common point of pride for many parents to see their children excel in both academics and athletics while in school. This was the case for the father of a student named Mawusimensah. The father's name was Ervin Mears, and he wanted his son to participate in his school's track race team (Sterling Regional squad). Unfortunately, his wishes were cut short after his son was kicked off of the track team. Mears decided to take multiple people to court over this, including the track coach, the school's principal, and multiple board members, demanding a whopping $40 million in damages. He accused the school and team of harassing and bullying his son and unfairly kicking him off the team without a valid reason.

The track coach rebutted the accusations by claiming that Mawusimensah missed too many practices, which is why he was removed from the team. Mears argued that these absences were a result of a death in the family and an injury to his son's leg. The court supported some of the claims raised by Ervin Mears but found that Mawusimensah was not racially discriminated against.

54

A DEADLY COUNTERATTACK

A video captured by a surveillance camera showed how a store owner shot a supposed robber. The robber, armed with a rifle, came into the Norco Market at 2:45 a.m. He pointed the gun at the owner, asking him to put his hands in the air. The owner had a hidden gun close to where he was attacked. In a matter of seconds, he got a hold of his gun and shot the suspect in the arm. The robber ran off screaming and shouting. Other cameras indicated armed men with weapons and face coverings entering the store together with the robber who was shot. Apparently, there were 3 or 4 gunmen. Another camera in the parking lot showed the suspects fleeing the store premises after the first robber was shot in a dark-colored BMW SUV.

A police report stated that four suspects were found at a hospital, with one of them injured by a gunshot and in critical condition. The four suspects were arrested and charged with robbery, conspiracy, and possessing stolen unlicensed guns. They were held together in police custody for a bail worth $500,000.

The 23-year-old robber who was shot, although facing criminal charges, sued the store owner who shot him. The police, in a report, said the store owner's gun was licensed, and he only tried to protect himself, his property, and his community from his attackers.

55

APPLE MADE THEM DO IT

In 2017, Chris Sevier sued the state of Utah for not allowing him to marry his computer. He filed similar lawsuits in three other states, but these were all overshadowed by his lawsuit filed against Apple. In a 50-page complaint, Sevier blamed Apple for his addiction to pornography. Aside from saying the company was the reason he could access pornography at all, he accused them of supporting and even promoting the consumption of pornography by not creating content filters for their internet browsers. Sevier wanted to see Apple apply restrictions to their internet browsers, which prevented underaged users from accessing inappropriate content, as well as to compensate him for the relationships damaged as a result of his porn addiction. Sevier faulted Apple for his failed marriage, emotional stress, and a multi-day hospitalization. Nothing came of the lawsuit, and Apple never responded to Sevier's demands to have more restrictions placed on the product browsers.

56

WHERE ARE THE GRANDBABIES?

Sanjeev Ranjan Prasad and Sadhana Prasad spent their life savings on their son's lavish wedding. In return, they demanded that their son and daughter-in-law conceive within a year of the wedding, or they would look for legal compensation. Six years passed, and still, the Prasads were without grandchildren, which led them to sue the couple for $65,000. The Prasads claimed that this was the cost of sending their son Shrey to aviation school. Even after receiving an education, the young man ended up relying on his parents for financial support for two more years until he was married. In addition to the expensive wedding, the parents paid for the honeymoon and a new car.

The plaintiffs added in a statement that they'd been patient enough but couldn't take it any longer. They affirmed that they had earlier left the decision of having kids to the young couple, but it seemed they didn't have any interest in having children. Their suit accused the son and his wife of mental harassment by depriving the parents of their dream of becoming grandparents. They described the son and daughter-in-law's actions to be very embarrassing and hurtful, especially when they see other people their age dropping off their grandkids at school.

57

THE END OF ELF TYRANNY

Elf on the Shelf has become a popular Christmas tradition. The toy doll and accompanying storybook come with a game that relies on parent participation. To keep the magic alive for children, their parents must move the elf each night, which can become a burden to some, with some families not having access to the toy and other parents just outright tired of the stress that comes with the elf. After Chief Judge Robert D. Leonard II suffered an experience where all three of his children were in tears after an incident where one of the kids "murdered" the Christmas elf, he set out to give other parents some holiday relief by creating a mock ruling. The Cobb Judicial Circuit Superior Court sent out a letter for parents to show their children, which banished all the elves from the county, claiming that they were a distraction from studies and a risk to the well-being of the children. Playfully, he tweeted that anyone who enjoyed their elf would not be held in contempt of the court.

58

BAKED IN THE WRONG STATE

At this point, it shouldn't surprise you to see lawsuits against major brand names regarding authenticity. This is exactly what happened with the parent company Kings Hawaiian bakery, when Robert

Galinsky took the company to court over their Hawaiian sweet rolls packaging.

Robert Galinsky filed a class-action suit at the federal high court of Manhattan against King Hawaiian bakery, claiming the company was misleading its customers by placing images of Hilo, Hawaii, on the rolls' packaging when they were really produced in California. Galinsky claimed it led the general public to believe the rolls contained traditional Hawaiian sweet roll ingredients such as honey and pineapple juice, and since they did not, they were really not Hawaiian-styled rolls at all. These were the grounds that led him to request the company to change its branding and to pay damages for misrepresenting its product in order to sell more rolls.

The Kings Hawaiian bakery rebutted by recounting its history. The company did start in Hilo, Hawaii, in the 1950s. It moved to Honolulu a decade later and finally changed its location to Torrance, California, in 1977, where it still makes its rolls. The company also drew attention to how this location, as well as a list of ingredients (not including pineapple or honey), were clearly printed on the packaging. After lengthy proceedings, the court decided to dismiss the case, siding with the bakery's defense that any reasonable person would see the product's details on the packaging before purchasing the product.

59

BATMAN FACES BATMAN

Christopher Nolan was the creator of the box-office hit *The Dark Knight*, a popular film in the Batman saga. However, he was taken to court, unaware that the popular comic shared the same name as an actual town in Turkey. In 2008, Hüseyin Kalkan, the mayor of Batman, sued the filmmaker along with Warner Bros production company for using the name without permission. According to the mayor, the use of the name had a major impact on the town, and it was believed to have contributed to a rise in the murder and suicide rate. In addition to this, residents attempting to move to other countries ran into repeated legal issues as the fictitious superhero popularity caused people to question the validity of the town name.

60

NOT ENOUGH
REAL BUTTER

In 2022, Rachael Barnett filed a complaint against Mrs. Smith's apple pie for its misleading packaging. On the box, it is printed clearly that the product is made with real butter in large letters, accompanied by a picture of a sliced stick of butter. Barnett was upset because, despite the boldly displayed selling point, the ingredients showed that the product only contained a "shortening butter blend," with its first ingredient of the blend being palm oil rather than butter. In addition to the blend, there was more palm oil in the crust's ingredients, which indicated that there was a lot of palm oil and only a small amount of actual butter.

Barnett felt as if she had been taken advantage of and misled by Mrs. Smith's advertising scheme. She claimed she would not have paid such a high price if it wasn't for the bold claims making it appear as if the crust was made in an old-fashioned and healthier manner. The plaintiff accused Mrs. Smith's of fraud and negligent representation and requested a jury trial with the hopes of receiving financial compensation, not only for herself but also for other customers misled by the product's packaging. As of the writing of this book, the case is still open, and anyone living in Illinois, Utah, Virginia, Wyoming, Arkansas, Ohio, Nevada, North Carolina, or Alabama is encouraged to join the lawsuit.

61

NOT ENOUGH CUPS

In 2022, Folgers CoffeeHouse products came under scrutiny when two separate class action lawsuits were filed against the company in two different states. Geoff Thompson of Texas and Julie Marthaller of Washington went to court with similar suits questioning Folgers's listed packaging claims. Although the numbers are different in both cases, the issues are the same. On Folgers's coffee canisters, the number of cups of coffee it says it makes does not match the actual brewed amount.

In Geoff Thompson's case, the package claimed that the 30.5-ounce container would make 240 cups of coffee, but he only made 203 servings. Marthaller bought a 25.4-ounce container that claimed to make 210 cups of coffee but only made 169 cups. In both these cases, the serving size is listed — each cup is defined as a 6-ounce cup of coffee.

These cases were represented by the same law firm and are requesting $5 million in damages — a high price for about 40 cups of coffee in each case. Part of the reason for such a high amount, though, is because these customers have bought the same product for years, not realizing they were paying for around 40 cups of coffee they didn't receive; chances are, many other people have experienced the same issue without being aware that the products are falling short.

62

A FRIGHTFUL EXPERIENCE

Most people anticipate a good scare when they attend a haunted house; however, rarely do they expect to come out actually injured. In 1999, Deborah Mays attended a House of Horrors put together as a fundraising event for Gretna Athletic Boosters Inc's programs. While in the haunted house, Mays was startled and ran into a wall that was covered in black plastic. The impact ended up breaking her nose, which required two corrective surgeries to fix. The woman argued that having black plastic and no lighting in that area was the cause of the accident, and although she knew she would become scared, she felt as if this was a dangerous combination that could also injure others. Unfortunately, the court dismissed the case stating that the plaintiff went into the House of Horrors expecting frightening experiences and that the accident was caused by abnormal reactions.

63

A GROTESQUE VENDETTA

In 2009, James Carroll Butler did something unthinkable to his coworker. The 53-year-old Virginia resident worked in a wastewater plant and had issues with his coworker, a mechanic named Michael Utz. Instead of filing a complaint with human resources, Butler decided to collect urine from one of the public toilets and use it in the work coffee pot, waiting patiently for Utz to indulge. The good news is that Michael Utz could smell the urine, and instead of drinking the coffee, he decided to take the entire pot to his boss, who promptly tested it. Butler was arrested for the misdemeanor and charged with one month of jail time and a year of probation. Utz took Butler to court, seeking $728,000. Although the court did not agree to this huge amount, they did give Utz $5,001 in damages.

64

A SMELLY SITUATION

La Jolla Cove, commonly known as the jewel of San Diego, was and still is home to luxurious houses, fine dining, and a serene beach. Unfortunately, this beautiful city is stained with sea lion feces. The smell is fierce enough that La Valencia Hotel and George's at the Cove filed a lawsuit against La Jolla Cove for failing to do anything in regard to the businesses' multiple complaints. They claimed the foul smell was driving off their customers, posing a health risk and creating a serious public nuisance. For two years preceding the lawsuit, the local businesses had attempted less drastic measures, trying their best to get help cleaning up the sea lion feces to no avail. The restaurant owner, George Hauer, claimed the town had promised to deal with the problem immediately when they complained, but they hadn't received any response from anyone after that. La Jolla Cove underwent similar issues in the past with animal feces and usually dealt with the problem by using a bacterial solution to dissolve the animal waste. However, these were for birds, not federally protected sea lions. This was why the case was initially dismissed. Despite residents and business owners looking for help to clean the feces from the area, the judge decided to focus on the animals themselves and decided that La Jolla Cove was not responsible for removing or scaring off the animals and would even come under legal scrutiny if they tried. When the local business owners tried to fight for help again, the judge decided he couldn't make the city enter a steeply-priced contract to clean the animal waste from the shores.

65

TABLE FOR ONE

In 2015, a woman named Kathleen Hampton was turned away from Enzo's Caffe Italiano on Valentine's Day. The Oregon resident booked a reservation for two in advance, but her husband canceled at the last minute. They had already eaten a large meal over a lunch date, and he did not think he was hungry enough for a five-course meal. Hampton still wanted to treat herself to the special meal designed by the restaurant, especially for the holiday. While already seated, she asked for a menu, and the waitress treated her rudely and told her she would not be served and needed to give up the table. Hampton believed this was because of racial discrimination. She took the story to the internet and later proceeded to sue the restaurant, requesting $100,000 and a public apology.

The restaurant owner and wait staff had a different perception of the events. Because of the high volume of customers on Valentine's Day, customers were only seated when their full party arrived. According to the wait staff, Hampton was not asked to leave the restaurant nor refused service—instead, since she was a party of one, she was asked to eat either at the bar or in the outdoor seating section. This was standard to make sure that the restaurant could keep up with the busy evening. In the end, Hampton decided to settle for an unknown amount and sign a privacy agreement, keeping the story from further tarnishing the restaurant's reputation.

66

A SPICY NEIGHBOR

The popular hot sauce Sriracha, produced by Huy Fong Foods, faced a major lawsuit when residents living near their factory in Irwindale, California, pressed charges. The hot sauce factory not only created a terrible smell but many of the locals also reported experiencing headaches and burning eyes. One family even complained that the smell was bad enough that they needed to move their outdoor birthday party indoors because no one could handle the stench. Some of the locals experienced symptoms as bad as bleeding noses and breathing issues. The lawsuit put pressure on the company to stop production and come up with a plan for protecting local residents from the smell. The factory refused to take action on its own, despite prompting from the city to do something to filter the air. If it is decided that the factory is a public nuisance, production could be shut down, or the factory could be forced to move to another location further from residential properties.

A DEADLY THREESOME

In 2009, 31-year-old William Martinez was scheduled for testing to investigate pain radiating from his chest and down his arm, which his doctor believed was caused by clogged arteries. A day before his testing, though, he ended up dying in a threesome.

Martinez's family sued the cardiologist for $5 million for not warning him to avoid any physical stress. They believed if the doctor had warned the deceased, he wouldn't have engaged in any activity that could cost him his life. The plaintiff's lawyer said Martinez's medical reports were poorly recorded, and the doctor didn't ask him to abstain from any stressors until after the test. Dr. Gangasani's attorney claimed Martinez was clearly instructed to abstain from any stressful activity until after the test. The court awarded the plaintiff $3 million instead of $5 million after determining that Martinez was 40% in control of his health. However, the defendant's attorney said they would appeal the verdict.

68

PAW CAUGHT
IN THE BEE HIVE

In 2008, a Macedonian beekeeper named Zoran Kiselosky pressed charges against a local bear. According to Kiselosky, someone was stealing honey from his hives, so he set up cameras and lights to catch the thief. Unfortunately, the perpetrator was a bear. At first, the beekeeper drove the bear off using "turbo-folk" music, which is known for its vibrating bass. This only worked for a few weeks before the generator running the lights and music ran out of power, and the bear returned to steal more honey. Because the bear was considered a protected animal, the courts charged the state with paying $3,500 worth of damages.

69

FARMER AT FAULT

Tony Martin, a 55-year-old farmer, was considered to be rather paranoid when it came to burglars. His house was booby-trapped, his windows barred, and multiple "lookouts" were built in trees surrounding his property. The man was known for often sleeping fully clothed, prepared for an unforeseen attack, and was well known for threatening to kill anyone who entered his farm unannounced.

In 1999, 16-year-old Fred Barras and 29-year-old Brendon Fearon attempted burglary on the property. Martin killed Barras and served time for the murder. When he was released, he faced a lawsuit pressed by Fearon for severe injuries he received during the burglary. Part of the dispute between Martin and Fearon revolved around the legality of Martin's weapon. It was clear that he owned the shotgun and ammunition with the full intent of injuring someone. Prior to the incident, it was reported that he repeatedly expressed racial discrimination against Fearon individually and against broad racial groups in general. Martin received five years in jail, Fearon received time for the burglary, and both Fearon's and Barras's families sought further compensation from Martin following his release.

TRAGIC TRAINWRECK

In 2008, a tragic train accident at Edgebrook Metra Station in Chicago killed an 18-year-old man named Hiroyuki Joho. Joho was running across the railroad tracks, unaware of the oncoming train. The locomotive crushed the majority of his body, but there were body parts thrown into the air, which, unfortunately, knocked down a woman named Gayane Zokhrabov, who was waiting on the opposite platform. Zokhrabov ended up with a broken leg, broken wrist, and severely injured shoulder. Due to the injuries incurred, Zokhrabov originally attempted to sue Joho. This was dismissed, as Joho was deceased; however, the case was revisited, this time looking to the train station to be held responsible for the injuries incurred on the platform.

DANGEROUS HEADLINES

Two gunmen attacked a printing shop in a suburb of Paris. The shooters were identified as Said and Cherif Kouachi. The siege led to the killing of 12 people who worked for Charlie Hebdo Magazine. One of the surviving employees, Lilian Lepere, hid under a sink throughout the shooting for over eight hours. He sued the printing company for revealing his whereabouts, which he believed endangered his life. He claimed that his whereabouts were made public both on different radio and television networks, and among them were two of France's largest television networks.

Although Mr. Lepere claimed that his whereabouts were made public, his exact location/hiding place was never mentioned. The shooters took Mr. Lepere's boss but later freed him, and the boss joined him under the sink until after the siege. His attorney, Antoine Casubolo Ferro, in a newspaper, said that giving out real-time information gave the armed men access to follow how their operation was going, and that was a risk for the plaintiff. None of the media houses responded to the claims.

72

NO RETURN POLICY

In 2001, Richard Batista, a Long Island surgeon, donated one of his kidneys to his wife, Dawnell, who needed the transplant to live. In 2005, Dawnell pressed charges against her husband and requested a divorce due to domestic violence and him cheating on her. After the trial was scheduled, Batista attempted to sue Dawnell, demanding she return the kidney he donated or otherwise pay him $1 million, which he claimed was what the kidney was worth. The argument was that the kidney was considered an item of marital property. The judge rejected the request, saying that since it was a human organ, it did not qualify as an item of marital property. Furthermore, he stated that Batista agreed to donate the organ legally with full consent, without any conditions stated under which he would request the organ back. The court warned him not to seek an appeal because he could end up facing charges of extortion and criminal prosecution.

73

AN UNNECESSARY SURGERY

In 2017, Wendy Ann Noon took the University of Kansas Hospital to court over a misdiagnosis and attempted cover-up. The previous year, Noon had been misdiagnosed with pancreatic cancer, which led her to have portions of her pancreas removed unnecessarily. When the mistake was discovered, instead of taking responsibility, the hospital proceeded to cover up the misdiagnosis. This led Noon to take legal action against the hospital, suing them for negligence and civil conspiracy. The doctor responsible, Meenakshi Singh, not only falsely claimed to have received a second opinion regarding the diagnosis but then proceeded to alter documents after the surgery was completed to try to hide it. Although Singh remained on the hospital's staff, the hospital was forced to pay Noon $1.8 million in a settlement. Aside from the personal loss experienced by the patient, the lawsuit revealed that the hospital put all its patients at risk during a federal investigation attached to the case.

A TIP WORTH FIGHTING OVER

Tonda Dickerson was the waitress on duty at Grand Bay Waffle House on March 7, 1999. As a tradition of the restaurant, all the tips given for that day belonged to her. Edward Seward, who ate breakfast there on that same day, gave his lottery ticket as a tip, which was something he often did. Little did Dickerson know that in a matter of weeks, her life would change forever. She got the lottery ticket tip on a Sunday, and the next draw was the following Saturday. She won a whopping sum of $10 million with the ticket Seward gave her. Like every other lottery winner, she was given the option to either take the lump sum or spread the payout over a 30-year period. She agreed to the latter option, where she would receive $375,000 per year over 30 years. Dickerson's happiness was cut short when she got involved in numerous legal cases with colleagues, friends, family, internal revenue, and Seward (who had given her the ticket).

Dickerson's colleagues filed a suit claiming that the money she won from the lottery should be shared equally among them. However, Dickerson argued that every waitperson took the tips she got on their workday without sharing and questioned why hers should be any different. Her lawyer said the coworkers just wanted to take advantage of her. The plaintiff also claimed that other coworkers had, in the past, received lottery tickets from customers. The court ruled that Dickerson's lottery win was worth a fraction of the actual value.

Three years after the lawsuit with her colleagues, Seward filed a case claiming that he had an agreement with Dickerson to buy him a truck if the ticket won.

75

PREMEDITATED EVIDENCE

Daniel Keith Ludwig was an American billionaire who made his fortune by developing one of the largest salt companies in the world. Ludwig married a woman named Gladys in 1928, and Gladys gave birth to a daughter named Patricia during their marriage. However, Ludwig claimed that the daughter was not his, and the couple ended up divorcing. Forty years after his death, Patricia challenged the billionaire's will, claiming she had a right to the inheritance because she was his biological daughter. Ludwig, concerned this may happen, had samples of his DNA preserved in the 1970s. When the DNA samples were compared to Patricia's, it was discovered that he was not her father, and the case was dismissed.

76

A WELL-DISGUISED FATHER

Paternity fraud is not uncommon; however, in most cases, it involves people who know each other. In 2009, Karen Sala sued actor Keanu Reeves, claiming that he was the father of her four children. As all four children were adults, she sought $3 million and an additional $150,000 for spousal and child support.

According to the actor's lawyers, the defendant tried to settle the dispute by carrying out a DNA test, and the result showed that none of the four children were his. However, Sala did not drop the case. Instead, she accused Reeves of tampering with the DNA test.

Sala claimed to have had a sexual relationship with the actor before, during, and after her marriage. She also claimed that she and Reeves lived together for a period of time and that he was present at some of the births of the children. Keanu Reeves stated he had never met the woman before in his life. When presented with this, Karen Sala told the court that Reeves had disguised himself as her ex-husband.

The defendant's lawyer asked the court to get Sala's ex-husband's DNA because their divorce documents claimed he was their father. He also wanted the children's birth certificates to be presented to the court. Sala refused both motions to provide her ex-husband's DNA test and the children's birth certificates. The court dismissed the case saying there were no triable issues or evidence to proceed with the lawsuit.

77

ALL-INCLUSIVE PORNOGRAPHY

A man Yaroslav Suris from Brooklyn, who is hearing impaired sued Pornhub for discriminating against people with disabilities. He claimed that the porn site had sidelined those with hearing impairment by not providing captions on their videos. He said his disability prevents him from understanding the audio, and the captions would be the only way to enjoy the videos like every other viewer. He filed a class action lawsuit against the company for violating federal law.

The plaintiff said the website should have included closed captions to give all viewers equal access to the content, and that included people with hearing disabilities. Suris's further said his love for porn made him subscribe to a premium package on Pornhub, but he wasn't getting value for his money. He wanted to access the millions of adult videos on the premium package and enjoy them. Without getting the satisfaction he felt he deserved, he was seeking compensatory damages and for the company to face other penalties for discrimination. It was discovered that there was closed captioning for the site's videos, which led to the dismissal of the case.

78

BUYER'S REMORSE

Trina Thompson took Monroe College of New York to court when the 27-year-old failed to find a job after graduating. She received a degree in Business Administration with a focus on information technology, which cost her $70,000 in tuition fees. The lawsuit requested that the school pay tuition costs plus an additional $2,000 for the stress incurred.

Thompson argued that she graduated with a 2.7 GPA, which should have led to employment. She also stated in her suit that the college had provisions to help students get a job; however, Thompson did not receive any help from their services. Trina Thompson put the responsibility on the institution to help her find work post-graduation. Although the case cost her nothing, the visibility it garnered in the media led to a job offer.

79

IT'S THE
REAL DEAL

The slogan on Barilla brand spaghetti reads "Italy's #1 Brand of Pasta." This bold slogan led California residents Mathew Sinatro and Jessica Prost to file a class action lawsuit against the pasta company under the pretense that they purchased the product believing that the pasta was made in Italy. In addition to the motto's statement on the box, it was framed by three leaves in green, white, and red, symbolic of Italy's flag. The argument was that they would not have paid such a high price for pasta if they did not believe it was authentic Italian pasta. The company responded by stating that the pasta sold by the company in Italy was made in Italy and that the pasta sold in the United States was made in the United States; however, the recipe for all their pasta was the same. The company requested that the case be dismissed.

NOT ENOUGH NUTRIENTS

In 2019, Victor Cardoso filed a class action lawsuit against Canada Dry Ginger Ale, accusing the company of making false claims about the health benefits of their product. He also blamed the company for misleading its customers. The plaintiff complained that he, his wife, and his daughter had been consuming the ginger drink because of its claimed health benefits. In the suit, he claimed that the packaging on the product clearly stated that it was made with natural ginger. The plaintiff's lawyer argued that the company's claims were false and misleading because the product didn't contain actual ginger.

The company argued that they use ginger concentrate in making the drinks. However, the plaintiff's lawyer argued that the company boils ginger in ethanol, which destroys all the nutritional benefits of the ingredient. After that, they only add 5ml of the boiled concentrate in a batch that could fill up 70 cans. He further said that even with the company's argument that they use concentrate, the health benefits they promised would be destroyed in the manufacturing process. Their claim and label of the product being made with natural ginger was false.

The case lasted for over 12 months before a British Columbian court settled for the plaintiff. The company was ordered to pay Cardoso $200,000. However, the company was not required to change its labeling or any advertisement. Because it was a class action suit, the attorneys took a $100,000 cut, and Cardoso and the other plaintiff got $1,500 each out of the money paid. Because the suit was a class action case, not all consumers could be located. Therefore, the remaining money was donated to a non-profit foundation in British Columbia.

81

A MONUMENTAL MIX-UP

In April 2014, William Cronnon ordered lunch at one of the Cracker Barrel branches in Marion County, Tennessee. He asked for a glass of water, and after taking a sip, he experienced a burning sensation in his throat and mouth. It was later discovered that he was given a glass of kitchen cleaning chemicals instead of a glass of water, which led him to file a lawsuit requesting $9.4 million in damages. There is a limit on how much a plaintiff can receive in damages, and Cronnon ended up only receiving $750,000 despite the life-threatening severity of the mistake. Ingesting the chemicals caused severe and permanent damage, including internal burns, and it was discovered that the restaurant was keeping the harsh cleaning solution in unmarked pitchers, which is how it was confused for water in the first place.

82

THE CHICKEN FINGER CLAUSE

Raising Cane, a restaurant franchise specializing in selling chicken fingers, signed a 15-year lease with a shopping center in Hobart, Indiana. The branch planned and started construction on a branch that included two drive-throughs and an outdoor patio, costing well over $1 million to build. It wasn't until construction was almost complete that the restaurant owners discovered that they were banned from selling chicken fingers on the premises, despite that being the only thing Raising Cane produces. This was due to a contract that the property owner held with the neighboring McDonald's. Raising Cane took the property owner to court, as they felt trapped in a 15-year lease.

Raising Cane argued that the shopping center misled them and hid important information during the lease negotiation. The defendant said the presence of McDonald's wouldn't conflict with Raising Cane's operation. However, the plaintiff argued that the defendant knew their business model revolved around chicken fingers. The defendant stated they had given Raising Cane the right to sell deboned chicken in the shopping center, but the plaintiff argued that the defendant had previously sold that right to McDonald's. In the end, Raising Cane was allowed to void the lease and received an unknown amount to cover the lost costs of construction.

83

TASTE THE TOXINS

In 2016, Mars candy makers were brought under scrutiny when it was discovered that their Skittles candy contained dangerous levels of titanium dioxide. The company made a public pledge that it would phase out the toxin over a five-year period. Six years later, Jenile Thames sued the company since there were still high levels of toxins in the candies. The lawsuit said the company had violated the California consumer protection law; therefore, they should pay for damages. Furthermore, Thames claimed she would have never purchased the candies, knowing they contained the harmful additive, which is the same chemical used in making paints, roofing materials, plastics, and adhesives. Without any public statement, Jenile Thames dropped the case before a verdict was passed.

84

SEEING DOUBLE

One of the most prolonged legal battles, starting in 1970 and lasting until 1977, was between Sid & Marty Krofft Television Production Inc and McDonald's Corporation.

In 1970, Needham, Harper & Steers, an advertising agency, pitched an idea to McDonald's, hoping for a collaboration. But before the McDonald's pitch, the agency had approached Sid & Marty Krofft, the brains behind the kids' live-action Pufnstuf.

Needham met the Kroffts to convince them to align their iconic Pufnstuf characters with the McDonald's campaign. In the end, both parties couldn't reach an agreement.

McDonald's welcomed the idea of Needham, and they aired their first McDonaldland commercial in 1971. Little did McDonald's know that this commercial would lead to one of their most extended legal battles. The Kroffts sued McDonald's for the striking resemblance between one of their characters, Mayor McCheese, and a character in Pufnstuf. The plaintiff said the resemblance was too obvious to be a coincidence. After the lengthy court battle, McDonald's lost the case and ended up giving the Kroffts an awarded sum of $1,044,000.

85

TOO COMMON
TO BE TAKEN

Taco John's was popularly known for the slogan "Taco Tuesday," which had a trademark for over 30 years. Having that trademark gave them the sole right to use it across the U.S., with the exception of

New Jersey. In New Jersey, there was a state-wide trademark that already existed, so they were the only state exempted. Over decades, Taco John's has sent a series of cease and desist letters to different businesses and companies using the same tagline. Taco John's filed a suit accusing Freedom's Edge Brewing Co. of using their trademark slogan. The lawsuit claimed that they had sent a cease and desist letter to the company earlier, but the company had failed to comply. The company continued using the slogan, and it had to go the legal route to protect its right to use the saying. Despite owning the trademark, the slogan has become a commonplace saying used by many establishments, which makes it a difficult situation both for Taco John's and any restaurant that uses the phrasing without knowing it is a trademarked term.

86

A RIGHT TO FAIR WAGES

Nusret Gökçe is a Turkish public figure most commonly known by his nickname, Salt Bae. The world-famous chef is known for his famous steakhouse, Nusr-Et. Many of the restaurant's employees filed a lawsuit against Salt Bae on account of their wages. The restaurant automatically adds an 18% gratuity onto their customers' bills; however, the employees thought it was unfair that this 18% counted as a portion of their wages instead of an addition to what they earned. Furthermore, Louis Pechman filed a separate lawsuit because he realized that the Miami and New York branches were being underpaid. In addition to this, the employees claimed they were not properly compensated for working overtime. The lawsuit ended with the court awarding Pechman and four waiters $230,000.

87

ALMOST AN
EVENT TO REMEMBER

In 2018, Kristen Yvette Martin was sued for scamming hundreds of people. The event promoter sold over $30,000 worth of tickets on social media for various food festivals that she never followed through with putting together. Although it appears she intended to create the events, having paid the deposit fee for a Crab Fest in Illinois, she never received the proper permits to fully host the events. Despite this show of intent, Martin's actions were deemed fraudulent. She was forced to pay $100,000 in damages.

88

FYRE FESTIVAL DISASTER

In 2017, tickets went on sale for an exclusive music festival. The ticket prices were in the thousands and boasted a Bahama all-inclusive retreat. Attendees were supposed to find personal villas, fine dining, live performances by famous artists, and the presence of many celebrities and models. Instead, people arrived on the island to find simple tents with rain-soaked mattresses and ham and cheese sandwiches. In addition to this, there were not even enough tents for the number of attendees. Many of the musicians canceled right before the event. Billy McFarland, CEO of Fyre Media, effectively scammed investors out of $26 million. After facing an incredible number of lawsuits and immense public outcry, McFarland was sentenced to six years in prison in addition to surrendering the $26 million he acquired through the fraud.

89

A HIDDEN COST

Robert Cameron went into *TGI Friday's* in Toms River, New Jersey, in August 2012, where he ordered his meal, a beer, a soda, and water. Little did *TGI Friday's* know that this simple order would land them a lawsuit after presenting the bill to the customer. After the meal, Cameron wasn't content with paying $5 for the beer and $3 for the soda. Because Cameron was dissatisfied, he filed a lawsuit against the restaurant, accusing them of not putting prices on their drinks. He claimed that if he had known the prices of what he was ordering, he would have opted for a cheaper beer and not bothered ordering any soda.

Cameron and his lawyer Sander Friedman believed that the restaurant had violated consumer fraud laws. The lawyer said the restaurant withheld the prices on the menu purposely so they could overcharge their customers. After the first court hearing in New Jersey, the lawsuit proceeded as a class action lawsuit, which allowed anyone who had purchased a menu item at *TGI Friday's* without a price clearly listed could join.

NOT ENCRYPTED ENOUGH

When Michael Alan Crooker's home was raided by the FBI, they gained access to his computers. Having suspected him of possessing explosive materials, they confiscated his technology, among other items. This led Crooker to file a lawsuit against Microsoft for failing to keep his information safe and secure. Crooker claimed in the lawsuit that he had protected his PC with an encryption mechanism to keep its data protected. However, the FBI and their team of cryptologists and electronic analysts broke through the protection, gained access to his hard drive, and found different types of pornographic content. The plaintiff said he was embarrassed that the FBI saw his privately kept belongings. In the lawsuit, Crooker said Microsoft software was meant to delete his browser history after every five days, but for some reason, the software had failed. He also said that an attendant for Hewlett-Packard at Circuit City (an electronic retail company) assured him that the deleted history was not recoverable when he was purchasing the PC. He claimed that the assurance Hewlett-Packard gave him was what further encouraged him to buy the PC. The plaintiff demanded compensatory and punitive damages from Microsoft worth $200,000. However, the case was thrown out because Crooker failed to pay a $250 filing fee.

91

GRUMPY CAT NOT AMUSED

Grumpy Cat became an internet sensation for its apparently bad-tempered expression. The cat, Tardar Sauce, went viral in different pictures where she made sour expressions. The images were first posted by the cat owner's brother on Reddit, where they quickly spread, and people began using them as memes. Because of the cat's popularity, Grenade, a coffee company in the U.S., signed a contract to use the cat's image to sell its product, "Grumppuccino." However, the cat owner filed a lawsuit after the company used the cat pictures to sell other products with Grumpy Cat apart from the one agreed on in their contract.

The original deal between Grenade Beverage and Grumpy Cat was worth $150,000. It was fully paid in exchange for the company's use of the cat's pictures on their iced coffee packaging. However, Grumpy Cat and her owner sued the company for a breach of contract.

In their lawsuit, the plaintiffs claimed the company exceeded their initial deal of using the image on just one product and, therefore, infringed their copyright and trademark. The defendant countersued, saying the cat and her owner didn't fulfill their end of the deal. Their lawyer further said the cat and her owner didn't mention the brand as much as they should on their social media platforms and TV appearances. In the end, a California jury ordered Grenade Beverage to pay the cat and her owner the sum of $710,000 for copyright and trademark infringement. They were also to pay $1 for breaching the contract.

92

NOT CLOSE ENOUGH

You have every right to be angry when you realize you're on your way to a destination contrary to that which you booked. A Maryland dentist, Edward Gamson, booked two tickets for his wife and himself to Granada, Spain. He had plans to visit the different historical sites of the city before going to an important work conference in Portugal. Little did he know that the agent he made a phone call with, stating he was booking for Granada, unfortunately, booked a flight to Grenada in the Caribbean.

Gamson argued in his suit that his e-tickets showed no duration or airport code, and there was no way he could have known there was a mistake in the booking. He mentioned in his lawsuit that he realized the error when the aircraft had a stopover in London. He was curious and asked one of the flight attendants why they were heading west since their destination was Spain. It was then the attendant told him they were headed to the West Indies, and this new discovery left Gamson wondering what had gone wrong. The plaintiff said he barely made it to his conference and suffered a loss for the hotel bookings, transport, and other tour arrangements he made for himself and his spouse.

The airline offered Gamson and his partner $376 and 50,000 miles each to compensate for the troubles they had endured. However, Gamson believed his loss was worth over $34,000 and sued the airline. British Airways at first attempted to move the case to a federal court where they could quickly get the case dismissed with the backing of international aviation rules. Unfortunately for them, the U.S. District Judge denied their request.

93

CLOSE ENOUGH
TO DRAW ATTENTION

MGA Entertainment, a California toy company, sued the luxury fashion company Louis Vuitton for interfering with sales for their Pooey Puitton product. The product is a children's purse featuring a poop shape filled with rainbow slime. MGA filed the lawsuit saying the luxury brand was criticizing and mocking their product in an attempt to intentionally decrease sales. Louis Vuitton, in return, accused MGA of copyright infringement. Since the purse sold for $58.99, MGA stated it was preposterous to conclude anyone would mistake the toy for a Louis Vuitton bag. In the end, the case was dismissed as the courts didn't think either claim was valid.

FIRST TO DIVERSIFY

Apple Inc. was sued for copyright by Katrina Parrott, the founder of Cub Clubs. Parrott filed a copyright lawsuit accusing Apple of infringing on the copyright of their app "iDiversions." The app was launched in 2013, and it was the first emoji app that offered different skin tones. However, Cub Club failed to provide tangible evidence to prove that Apple infringed and violated their property rights.

Parrott argues that the company had met with some representatives from Apple in 2014 to discuss the possibilities of becoming partners, but the two parties couldn't reach an agreement. Parrott claimed that it was after the failed partnership that Apple created a similar app to iDiversions. Apple's imitation also features options to use emojis in five different skin tones and other important features.

The judge, in his verdict, said Apple could not be charged with infringement because Cub Club had no protected trademark right for their app's emojis. Also, he stated that Apple's version of the emoji app was not similar enough to accuse them of infringement. He further said there were not many ways to express some emoji designs and shapes. With that, the judge dismissed the case in favor of Apple Inc.

95

NO ROOM FOR NAME DROPPING

Jelly Belly candy filed a lawsuit in Sacramento against David Klein for using the name "Jelly Belly." The defendant, who wasn't the founder, claimed to be the founder of Jelly Belly. The candy company, famous for its jelly beans, said that although they had some affiliation in the past with Klein, he had no right to portray himself as the company's founder. The lawsuit stated that, indeed, Klein came up with the company name in 1976. When Klein hired them, they were known by the name "Herman Goelitz Candy Company," and they produced gourmet jelly beans. Klein used the name Jelly Belly from 1976 to 1980. However, the plaintiff said they had some misunderstanding, and they acquired the "Jelly Belly" name from Klein for $4.8 million in 1980. After that, they ensured the name was trademarked so that Klein would not be affiliated with it in the future. The lawsuit said that even when they were affiliated with Klein, they were the manufacturers of the candies, and the only thing that changed from then was the name that they rightfully acquired.

96

UNWANTED SWEETNESS

A California woman, Jessica Gomez, filed a lawsuit accusing the candy company Jelly Belly of using false phrases to market their products. In 2017, Gomez purchased Jelly Belly's "Sport Beans," which were advertised as a health product designed for athletic recovery. The issue Gomez raised was that instead of listing sugar as an ingredient, they labeled it "evaporated cane juice," which led the average person to misinterpret the ingredient as a healthier substitute for sugar.

The counterargument made by the company was that the grams of sugar were listed on the nutrition label, which should be enough for customers to glean how much sugar they were consuming despite the clever wording in the ingredients list. Furthermore, Jelly Belly questioned if Gomez was even a real person and, if she was, whether she even purchased the product. Their reasoning for this was that there were no specific details listed in the lawsuit, such as where Gomez purchased the Sports Beans. On this note, Jelly Belly requested the case be dismissed. Gomez responded by moving the lawsuit to a federal court.

97

HARD HITTING FLY-BALL

In 2014, New Jersey resident Dana Morelli sued the Boston Red Sox baseball team after she was struck by a rogue baseball while attending a game. The Boston Red Sox were playing against the Milwaukee Brewers when a foul ball struck Morelli in the face. The impact caused the plaintiff to need three surgeries, and afterward, she still suffered pain from the incredible impact. Aside from the physical damages, Morelli brought up the fact that there were no safety measures in place to protect onlookers, which was negligent. The owner of the Boston Red Sox, John Henry, was forced to pay $9.5 million in damages. Since then, Fenway Park, where the ball game took place, has since taken measures to help protect its audience from future fly-balls.

HAND OVER
THE BACK PAY

Exotic dancers Sabrina Hart and Reka Furedi sought legal aid when they sued their employer, Rick's Cabaret, in 2014. The two dancers represented nearly 2,000 other exotic performers in court when they sued the strip club for withholding some of their earnings. The corporate owners, Rick's Cabaret International, Peregrine Enterprises, and RCI Entertainment, were all taken to court after failing to meet the local minimum wage and labor laws. The performers were looking for compensation in the form of back pay as well as stolen credit card tips they received for their performances. Despite lengthy battles, the exotic dancers won more than $10 million in damages.

99

DON'T BLAME
THE WEATHERMAN

Most people are aware that weather forecasts are not completely accurate. Despite this common knowledge, an unnamed Israeli woman sued her local news station for incorrectly predicting the weather. Danny Rup, the forecaster, was taken to small claims court after predicting sunny weather when it ended up raining. The woman who filed the lawsuit dressed for warm weather and ended up sick, which she argued was caused by the unforeseen storm. This caused her to miss multiple days of work, and she had to pay for medications to treat her illness. She sought $1,000 in compensation for the mishap. In the end, the most she received was a public apology for her suffering.

100

LOOKING FOR
DIVINE JUSTICE

Oddly enough, multiple people have attempted to sue god(s) for various grievances in multiple countries. Below are a few of the cases which made their way into courts. Some of them lost, and some of them surprisingly won. There are many other cases like these recorded throughout history, but here are some of the more interesting.

In 2016, a lawyer named Chandan Kumar Singh attempted to sue the Hindu God, Rama, for mistreating his wife, Sita. His aim was not to receive monetary compensation but a public awareness that the God was unfair to his wife. In 2007, a Romanian named Mircea Pavel attempted to sue God for fraud. He claimed that God failed to answer his prayers when he was sentenced to 20 years in jail for murder. Both of these cases were dismissed.

In 1969, Betty Penrose's house was struck by lightning, and her boss, a lawyer named Rusell Tansie, took God to court for damages to the lost home. Oddly enough, this case actually won on account of some legal loopholes. At the time, a hippie commune in California had given the deed to their land to God, which by all legal means, was the rightful owner. The argument was that if God owned land legally, he could also go to court. When no representatives showed up on behalf of God, the case was won by default, and Rusell Tansie won the $100,000 in damages for the destruction of Penrose's home.

101

NO PANTS
IN THE OFFICE

When police officer Jose Dones was taking his pants on and off, he never thought his actions would land him a lawsuit. Dones had repeatedly removed his pants while at the office, which made one of his female colleagues, Kelly Neal, uncomfortable. She reported this to their superior, but no action was taken, nor did they warn him to stop the unwanted behavior. With no help handling the situation, Neal decided to take the case to court.

The plaintiff complained in her suit that when she told her superiors about Dones's behavior, instead of them questioning Dones, she was the one punished. She was demoted and asked to return to street duty. Neal said the defendant had formed a habit of changing into different pants in the middle of the office when they had a locker room and bathroom for changing. Neal and other female officers became uncomfortable with Dones's behavior and complained, but he didn't make any adjustments. Along with the suit, Neal provided some video recordings she made of Neal exhibiting his character for the court to use as evidence.

It took a week before Dones's attorney responded and represented him in court. The attorney said the videos Neal presented to the court were recorded without the defendant's consent, which was a violation of the law. Dones's attorney, Angela Lee Velez, also said the defendant's actions were not malicious because he simply changed his pants without calling anyone's attention to himself.

CONCLUSION

There are many strange lawsuits that have found their way to court. Some are frivolous complaints of too much slack-fill or misrepresentation of ingredients, while others are more baffling, such as the cases taken to court against God or victims of crimes. The law has given everyone the right to seek justice when they feel their rights are violated.

Some of these lawsuits are indeed outrageously weird, but to the plaintiffs, they sought justice for what they believed was right. This book was designed to entertain its readers with these strange cases that saw their day in court.